how can fresh expressions emerge?

Share booklet 01

This *Share booklet* is one of a series which aims to encourage discussion about fresh expressions of church, without telling you what to do.

01 how can fresh expressions emerge?

02 how should we start?

03 what should we start?

04 how can we get support?

05 how can we find our way?

06 how can we be sustainable?

07 how can we be a great team?

Contents

Go out and stay out	3
A worship-first journey	4
A fresh expressions journey	5
Unpacking *a fresh expressions journey*	8
Moving from 'listening' to 'exploring discipleship'	12

Go out and stay out

Growing a fresh expression of church is not about starting church in a similar culture to our own in order to draw people into the ways of traditional church. Instead it is about incarnational mission, loving and serving people in their own context and 'being' church wherever that may be.

The start of the journey

Society has changed at a dizzying rate in recent years - thanks to a major shift in cultural attitudes and the ways in which we communicate with each other.

What was once the 'norm' has become an exception, including any involvement with Christianity. Today nearly 60% of the UK population finds it almost impossible to connect with church as we usually know it.

Many Christians are now tackling that challenge by developing fresh expressions of church to go out to where people are - and stay there.

But how might a fresh expression emerge? This booklet will help you to think about how the fresh expressions journey can start.

Two possible frameworks

New churches come to birth in many different ways. There is no 'right' approach.

Let us take a look at two contrasting frameworks to help pioneering teams discuss what sort of approach they might be called to and where they might be in the process of starting a new church. We recognise that there are - and will be - many variations from the pathways presented.

The first is **a worship-first journey**, which over the years quite a few churches have adopted, sometimes with fruitful results.

For the 'scarcely' or 'never churched' in particular a different tack may be required, something which we call **a fresh expressions journey**.

A worship-first journey

A large team or congregation is planted, often in a church building threatened with closure. The church plant offers worship and/or preaching as a shop window and members invite their friends to give it a go.

Rapid results?

A variety of events, such as presentations and discussions on contemporary issues, encourage these friends to explore the faith and attend an Alpha, Christianity Explored or Emmaus-type course, where they make a commitment. As a result they join a small group and get more involved in the church's life.

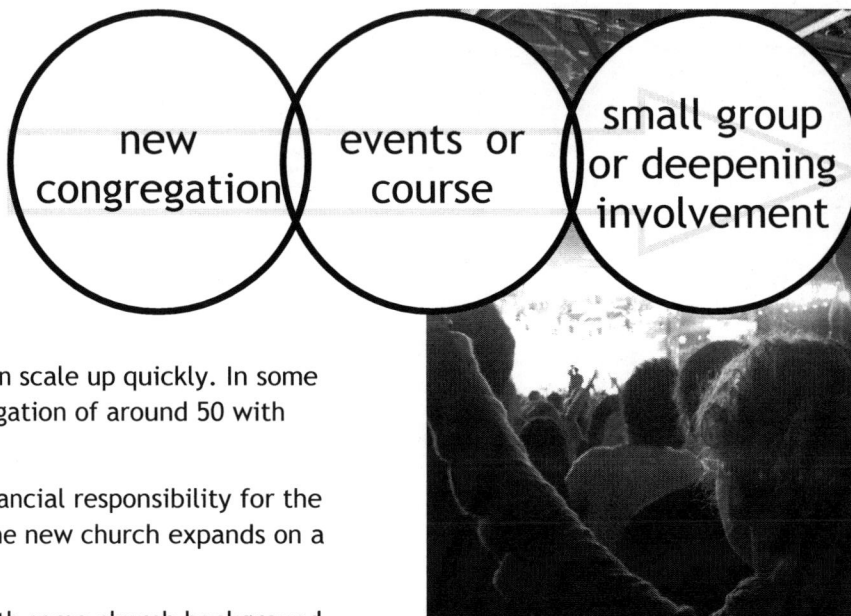

The great advantage is that the planting team can scale up quickly. In some versions, a large church might send out a congregation of around 50 with two or three paid staff.

As the congregation grows, it rapidly assumes financial responsibility for the staff and adds to their number. The mission of the new church expands on a self-sustaining basis.

This appears to work especially among people with some church background who have stopped attending and where members of the new congregation have good networks and are using them. But it is less effective in reaching people outside those networks who have difficulty in identifying with the congregation's culture, especially if they have little or no Christian experience. One pioneer who unsuccessfully tried a worship-first approach among young people with hardly any church background later remarked, 'Why would they come?'

In some contexts the two might be combined. A worship-first journey might give birth to a sizeable congregation, which in time asks 'Whom have we not reached?' A fresh expressions journey could then be used to connect with those who are not coming to the new church.

 expressions: making a difference
Fresh Expressions, 2011
Chapter 11: King's Cross Church

DVD

A London church planted a new congregation into King's Cross.

Chapter 25: 3.08 @ Kingshill

3:08 @ Kingshill is an example of a worship-first church plant that failed to attract those outside the church in significant numbers.

A fresh expressions journey

This starts with listening to God and to the people the pioneering team feels called to serve. The team begins to build loving relationships and engage in acts of service, as Jesus did.

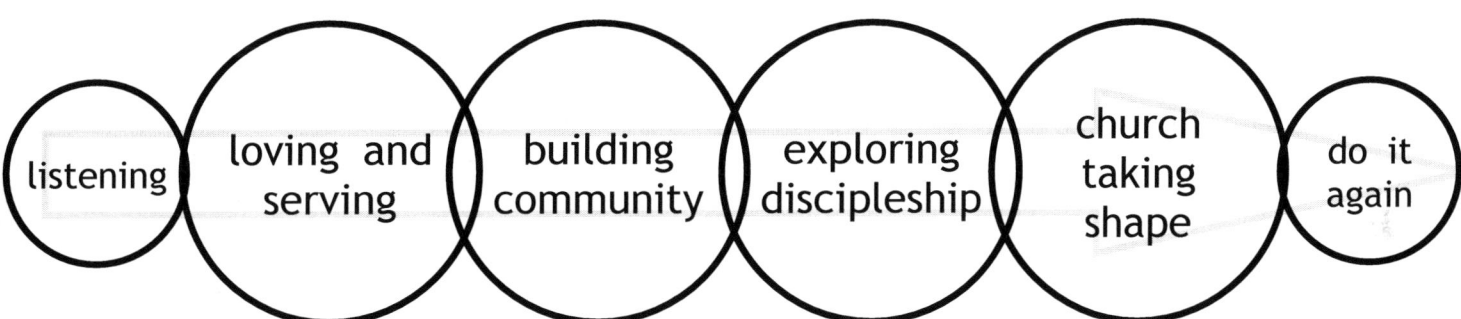

listening → loving and serving → building community → exploring discipleship → church taking shape → do it again

underpinned by prayer, ongoing listening and relationship with the wider church

Framework of trust

Loving relationships and acts of service might range from a spirituality-at-work group, to hanging out with friends, to a 'Saga group' for the over 50s.

Community develops as members of a drop-in centre, an environmental campaigning group or a discussion-over-curry group get to know each other, trust one another and develop a sense of belonging.

'Building community' is valuable in its own right. It is what Jesus did as he ate meals with his followers, travelled with them and devoted periods of special time to them. But it is also important for mission. Loving relationships reveal something of Christ, they give people a partial (though important) experience of church and they create a framework of trust within which to share the Gospel.

Low-key evangelism may continue throughout the initial 'stages', but as the need arises more intentional opportunities will be provided to explore becoming a disciple of Jesus. These could include mentoring individuals on a one-to-one basis. One person may be followed by another, till there is a sufficient number to form a small cell.

Or there could be enough people to form an explorers' group. The pioneering team might use or adapt a published course, or develop its own material. Or it might follow the example of one person who invited her friends to explore spirituality: 'Jesus is known as one of the world's greatest spiritual teachers. Why don't we look at the stories he told and see if we agree with them?'

Some people may come to faith quickly, but for others it will be very gradual. Patiently fanning the fire of the Spirit is a key task for the pioneering team. Once individuals start to believe, they should be encouraged to see discipleship as a life-long process affecting the whole of their lives.

As people begin to enter faith, they will consider what it would mean for them to be church in their culture. Church shaped by the gospel and their culture will emerge round them.

Emerging cells may cluster together in monthly or occasional meetings to provide a larger experience of church. Some will strengthen the spiritual life of the original group from which they came so that the group as a whole becomes more like church.

An Alpha cell might take responsibility for future Alpha courses, designed for people in the wider group. A luncheon club, influenced by a group of new Christians, might incorporate Holy Communion from time to time.

What is church?

Church is what happens when people encounter the risen Lord. At its heart are four sets of relationships:

- **UP relationships with the holy Trinity;**
- **OUT relationships in serving the world;**
- **IN relationships of deepening fellowship within the gathering;**
- **OF relationships in being part of the whole body of Christ.**

Though more is involved, we see church whenever we see these four sets of relationships forming around Christ, who is revealed in Scripture and celebrated in the sacraments.

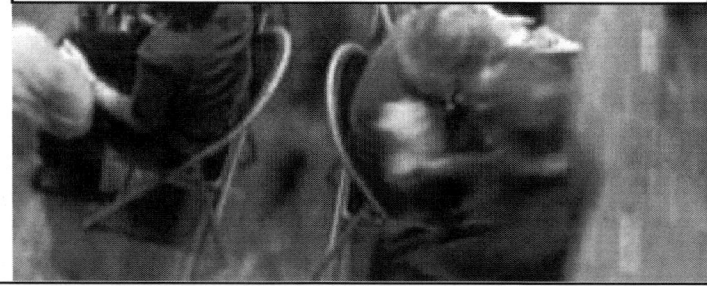

As church takes shape, it will reach out to and serve its context. One of its fruits will be to reproduce itself - to 'do it again' in a style that fits the context is a vital part of what it means to be church.

While the team may have seen this as church from the beginning, those being drawn into faith will grow only gradually in their understanding of themselves as being church. Leaders in the denomination may encourage and support the embryonic church from the beginning, but properly delay permanent recognition till there is evidence of stability.

The Sunday Sanctuary

Story

In 2009, St Luke's, Somerstown, felt that it wasn't reaching the people of their area in Portsmouth. At that time there were about 20 people in the congregation.

Vicar Mark Rodel put forward a proposal to the PCC for the church to move out and relocate to a community room in the Wilmcote House housing block. St Luke's would become The Sunday Sanctuary. It met with a mixed reaction but the proposal was approved. They did not set out to have a worship-first journey by creating a church service in a new setting, but started on the fresh expressions journey in order to meet new people, make friends and share stories.

The initial idea was to have something akin to a 'drop-in' for a couple of hours during which time breakfast would be available. Since then it has become more structured and focuses on engaging with a Bible story. There is no sung worship as such though time is set aside for praying in creative ways.

The move involved a lot of commitment in time, resources and energy from the congregation but they have already doubled the number of people that attended the original St Luke's. The Sunday Sanctuary is still in the process of building and deepening community life but members are beginning to explore discipleship in terms of what they do together. They original community - and the newer members - see themselves as all being evangelised by this process, reshaped by the gospel as they encounter it in new ways and with new people.

Unpacking *a fresh expressions journey*

The journey describes not how individuals find Christ, nor how the internal life of the pioneering team might evolve, but the action the team takes to enable a new expression of church to emerge.

Moving to the middle

The journey is the process encouraged by the team to help people move from the edge of the circle in the diagram to the centre. Whether the team is two or three people or larger, the internal and public aspects of the team's life are different.

The internal dimension is about what the team does to prepare for and bring to birth a new expression of church. Like conception, what is within the team - the church in embryo - will grow into the whole. The spiritual life of the team will shape the fresh expression as it develops. That is one reason why team relationships should be a priority.

The public aspect of the team's life, which is the journey, is about what prayerfully results as the team engages in mission.

The journey is a sequence of overlapping circles. Overlapping is important because it conveys something of the messiness of real life. 'Loving and serving' and 'building community', for example, may be so tied up together that they happen almost at the same time. Though simultaneous, they nevertheless may be distinct processes.

A language cafe may serve afternoon tea and encourage women from immigrant families to learn English by giving them topics to talk about at their tables. This is 'loving and serving'. 'Community' might be encouraged by suggesting that the women sit at the same tables for a few weeks so that they can get to know each other.

As each circle of the journey (page 4) kicks in, it remains present throughout the journey - 'loving and serving' don't stop. But the focus shifts from one circle to the next as the journey develops. The journey may be travelled quickly, but will often take a few years.

 Michael Moynagh, Andy Freeman
Share: How can we be a great team? (07)
Fresh Expressions, 2011

Book

Phil Potter
The Challenge of Cell Church
BRF, 2001

Eleanor Williams
Fresh Expressions in the Urban Context
YTC, 2007, p87

Barbara Glasson
Mixed-up Blessing
Inspire, 2006

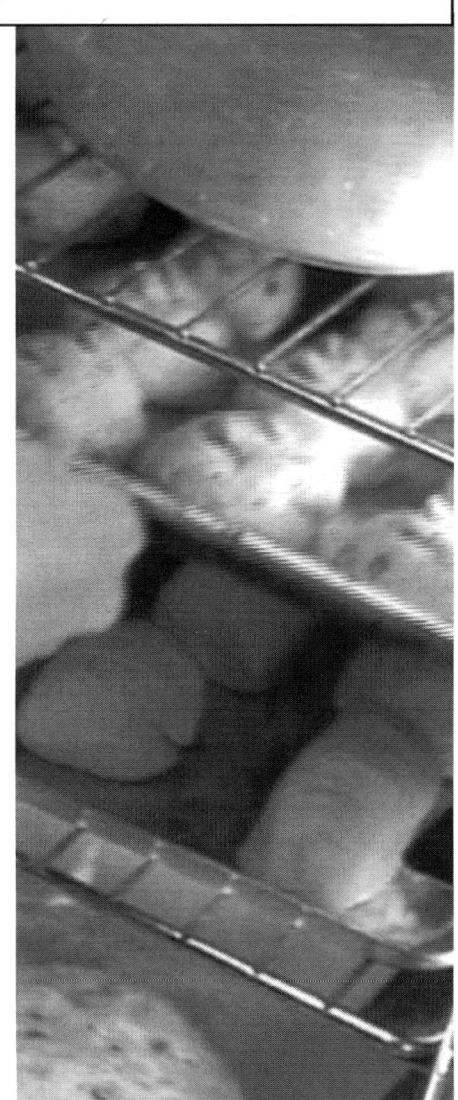

Some pioneers use different language or the four circles. Phil Potter, an experienced pioneer in Liverpool, encourages lay Christians:

> *...to share your passion, share your life, share your faith, share their journey.*
> **Phil Potter**, The Challenge of Cell Church, BRF, 2001

In her study of urban fresh expressions, Eleanor Williams suggests a sequence of blessing, belonging, believing, behaving. If we replace behaving with 'being church', this would map well on to our succession of circles.

Barbara Glasson's account of her experiences in *Mixed-up Blessing* is a good Methodist example of what we describe. She began by walking the streets of central Liverpool for a year, watching and listening. With a group of friends she began baking bread, giving the loaves away. Others began to join this loving and serving core. As they made the bread, community began to form.

> *Side-by-side encounters are infinitely less threatening than face to face ones.*
> **Barbara Glasson**, Mixed-up Blessing, Inspire, 2006, p39

In the middle of the day a period of quiet reflection was held in a side room. A Bible passage might be read and people were invited to comment, but not interrupt each other. There was space for silent prayer and reflection. Here was an opportunity for people to explore the Christian faith if they wished. Church gradually took shape.

We can discern a similar journey in the ministry of Jesus. Luke shows him teaching, healing and performing exorcisms in the early part of his public ministry. Then, while this loving and serving continues, there is a new focus on the call of the disciples (Luke 5.1-11, 6.12-16). Jesus is forming community, he describes his followers as his family (Luke 8.19-21). Building community presumably persists alongside his public ministry, but the focus falls more heavily on the process of making disciples - for example, sending out the 12 and 72, and the last supper. Luke describes how church takes shape in his second volume, the Acts of the Apostles.

We don't want to push this sequence too far. Not all fresh expressions grow in this way, especially among the scarcely or never-churched - the Spirit cannot be boxed into a single model. There will be times when the circles are taken in a different order or perhaps get missed out altogether. A fresh expressions journey is therefore both a simplification and a generalisation. You may ask how it fits your experience - might you adapt it or develop an alternative to describe what you are prayerfully expecting to do?

Sometimes, if you peer beneath an apparent exception to the journey, you will find that the journey's sequence is secretly at work. Some university students, for instance, may decide to run Alpha as an apologetics course. They might seem to be starting with exploring discipleship, but look closer. By starting with listening and prayer, they may have discerned that this was the best way, in their situation, to love and serve their fellow students.

Maybe they redouble their efforts to be good and generous friends to their peers. They want Alpha to spring out of a network of loving relationships and their invitations to get a favourable response. Though Christian apologetics is certainly present, during the first evening or two the focus is on building community - through the welcome, the meal, the discussion and much else. The hosts want people to feel at home and come back. Later, although the community dimension remains, attention shifts to encouraging individuals to explore discipleship and make a response. A follow-up course might be the context in which church begins to take shape.

Recognising this (or some other) journey can help you to be more intentional about it. You may be doing some things like building community intuitively. But seeing this as part of an overall process may encourage you to give it particular attention - and ask, 'could we do more to strengthen community?'

St Laurence, Reading

St Laurence, Reading is a church with a mission focus on young people that was started in 2001 and provides a good example of *a fresh expressions journey*. It came into being after leaders started to listen to students at local schools, hearing about their concerns and ideas.

By 2010 it had nearly 50 young people growing in the Christian faith, few with any previous church experience.

But this is far from an 'overnight' success story. A key moment for the church was when the local bishop, Stephen Cottrell, suggested a framework for thinking about what they were doing. Chris Russell and his fellow leaders had been doing more and more things to make contact with young people, and had some great relationships. But in terms of young people coming to faith the fruit was hard to come by; they were seeing hardly any teenagers take definite steps in following Jesus.

Bishop Stephen's framework (right) helped the leaders to become more intentional about what they were doing.

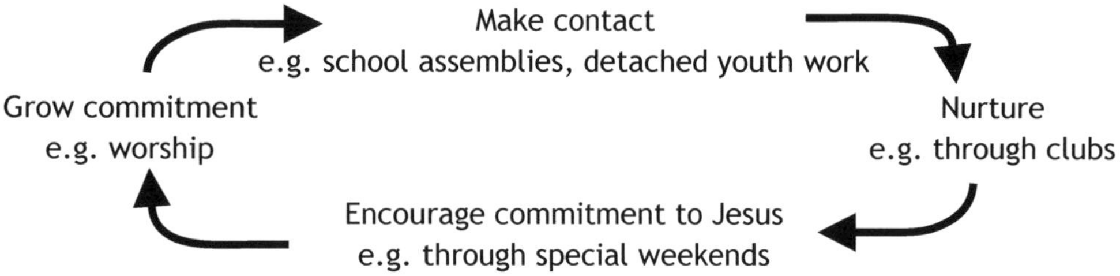

Make contact involves building relationships and engaging in simple acts of service. **Nurture** has

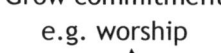

Make contact
e.g. school assemblies, detached youth work

Nurture
e.g. through clubs

Encourage commitment to Jesus
e.g. through special weekends

Grow commitment
e.g. worship

building community at its heart. A variety of clubs attract teenagers not mainly through activities but because the young people want to belong. As they enter the faith and **grow in their commitment**, church takes shape around them.

This structure has encouraged the leaders to ask of any activity, 'What happens next?' and to consider whether any of the steps from one 'stage' to the next is too big. For example, they are planning a 'Nurture 2' to turn the leap from 'Nurture' to 'Encourage commitment' into two shorter steps. Far from being a constraint, the framework has helped them stay creative but in a strategic manner.

Moving from 'listening' to 'exploring discipleship'

You may see clearly how to 'love and serve' and 'build community' but how do you encourage people to dig deeper and find out more about what it means to be a disciple in today's society? Appropriate evangelism is the answer. Understood in a broad way, it can be a vehicle for the Spirit to travel with people through the circles.

Acts of kindness can be especially powerful.

If people are to see Jesus, they must see his heart of love, which is best shown through generous relationships.

A lads and dads football team might support a lone parent family in their area. A book club with a spiritual dimension might provide financial support for a school library in Uganda.

Many people struggle to be as good as they want to be. Belonging to a group that has an altruistic dimension may help them achieve some of the goodness they aspire to.

As their hearts are warmed by being associated with something good, they may become more committed to the group and be more open to exploring what it means to follow Christ.

expressions: making a difference
Fresh Expressions, 2011
Chapter 09: Grafted

Grafted shows real kindness and practical support at their weekly drop-in centre.

God talk is about sharing your faith naturally in ordinary conversations and through events that provoke questions about Jesus.

These events may include opportunities for people to hear personal stories about faith. A leisure centre club for women featured talks by people who faced challenging circumstances, such as bereavement or raising a child with a disability. Because the speakers were Christians, they invariably described how God had helped them.

Guests always left with a bunch of flowers. People arriving at the leisure centre often asked, 'Where did you get those?' and were invited to the next meeting!

Missional worship is our phrase for what Ann Morisy calls 'apt liturgy'.

It is designed for people who have little faith or are confused about faith. It provides opportunities for encounters with God that heighten spiritual awareness and encourage individuals to explore Jesus.

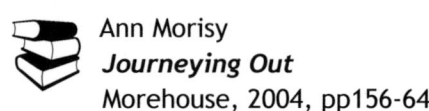 
Ann Morisy
Journeying Out
Morehouse, 2004, pp156-64

For instance, leaders of a retired persons' lunch group might put candles on the tables after the plates have been cleared away, play some Christian music, invite someone to read a few verses from the Bible, allow time for silent prayer and ask someone else to read a couple of written prayers - all lasting about 20 minutes. Guests could leave straight after lunch or stay behind for this simple act of worship.

Some church-run cafes have adjacent quiet rooms, perhaps with lighted candles, where individuals can pray and reflect silently. A prayer board played a key role in encouraging women of different ethnicity and backgrounds to talk about spiritual questions.

expressions: making a difference
Fresh Expressions, 2011
Chapter 05: CoffeeCraft

CoffeeCraft, in Clee Hill, use a prayer table at their weekly sessions.

Some who have run Alpha courses among people with little church background testify to the key role of worship. Worship can be quite 'full on' in some contexts if it is led sensitively.

As church begins to take shape, missional worship can evolve into a fuller expression of Christian worship.

The experience of healing can play an important part in opening individuals to God.

In a culture that strongly values experience, healing can give people an experience of God. Healing may come through the love of Christian friends, the prayer of Christians (in their personal devotions or corporate worship), healing services or through other kinds of prayer ministry.

Some people have called it power evangelism, while for others it is much more low-key. Avoiding unrealistic expectations is clearly important.

Creative expressions of spirituality can help to increase a group's awareness of spiritual issues.

Members of a group might be invited to express their spiritual longings and understandings through painting, photography, poetry, pottery and in other creative ways.

These might not be explicitly Christian, but frequently they will be pointers to God. As talking points, they may help others to feel more comfortable in expressing their spiritual views and to explore their beliefs.

Conclusion

Throughout the journey it is important to keep listening to God and the people you are serving, and to remain well connected to the wider church. After all, as individuals come into faith they will be baptised into the whole body of Christ.

The pioneering team needs to model this very distinctive Christian identity.

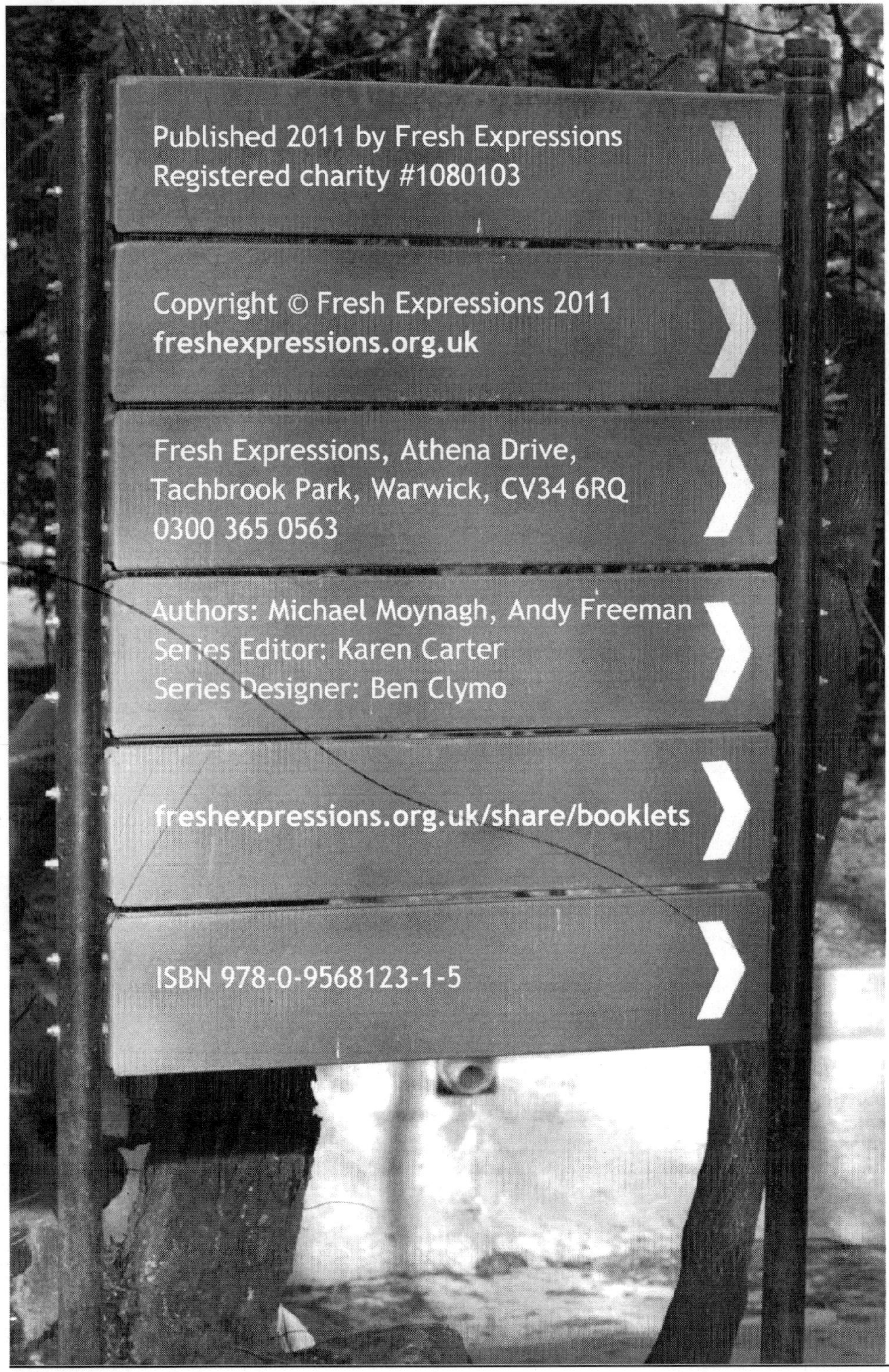

Published 2011 by Fresh Expressions
Registered charity #1080103

Copyright © Fresh Expressions 2011
freshexpressions.org.uk

Fresh Expressions, Athena Drive,
Tachbrook Park, Warwick, CV34 6RQ
0300 365 0563

Authors: Michael Moynagh, Andy Freeman
Series Editor: Karen Carter
Series Designer: Ben Clymo

freshexpressions.org.uk/share/booklets

ISBN 978-0-9568123-1-5

Related resources

expressions: making a difference
(Fresh Expressions, 2011)

 A DVD containing 28 stories illustrating the lessons to be learnt as fresh expressions of church make a difference to people's lives.

Available from
freshexpressions.org.uk/shop

sharetheguide.org

 An online resource including a guide to fresh expressions, community, blog and learning networks.

freshexpressions.org.uk

 Further stories and information, plus audio and video material and resources to download and purchase.